MAMA Wi
Your Baby's First Word

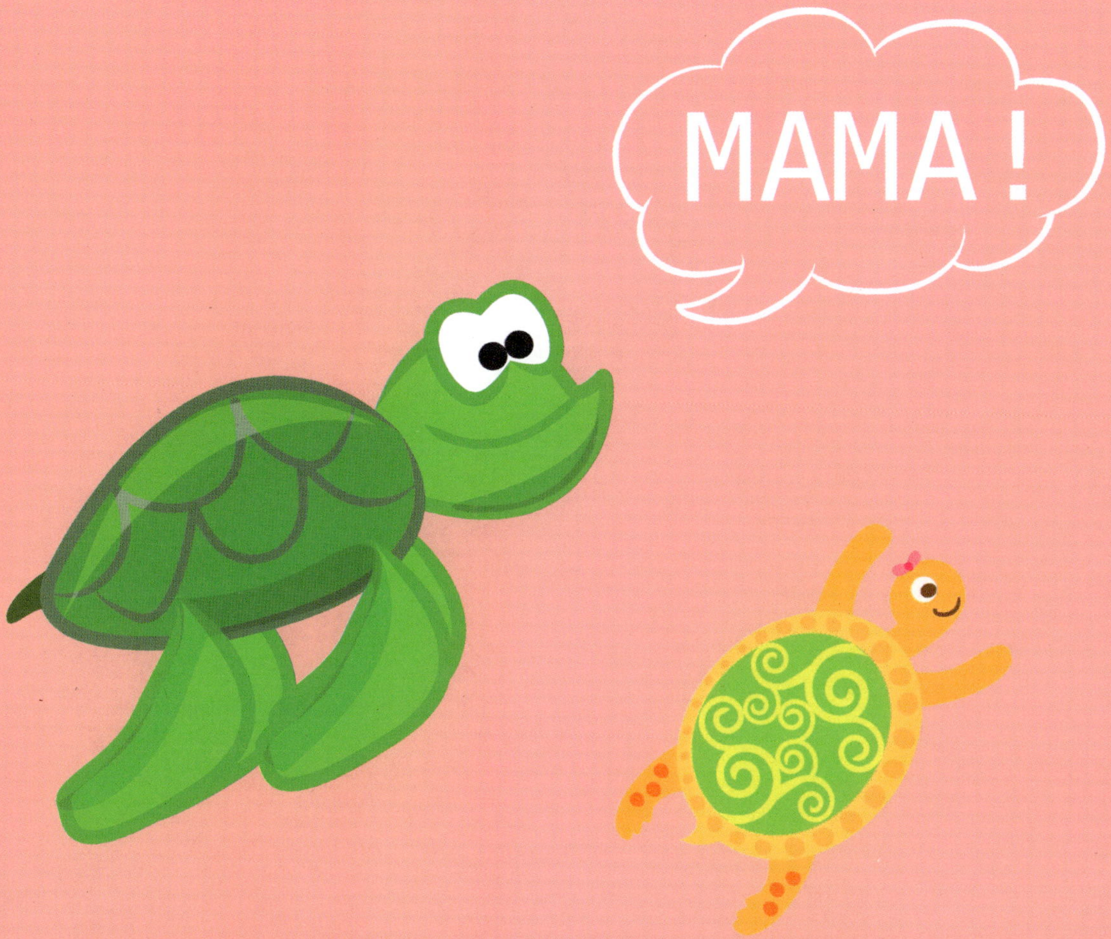

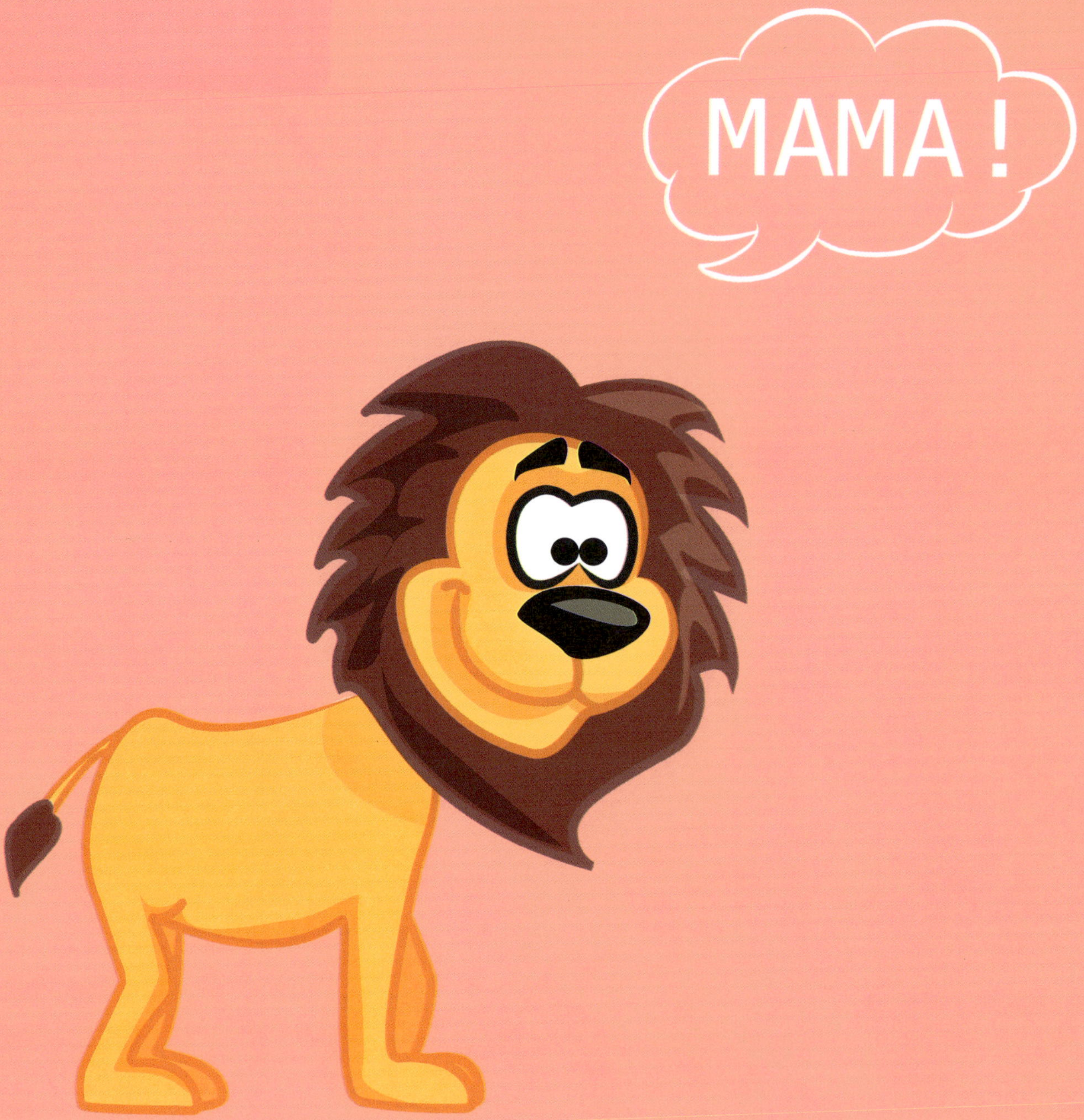
MAMA !

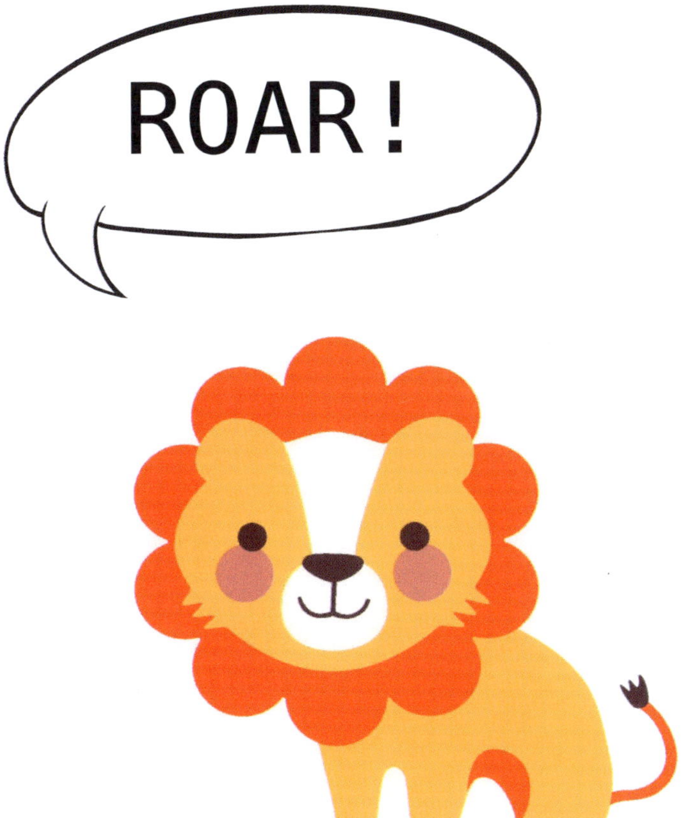
ROAR !

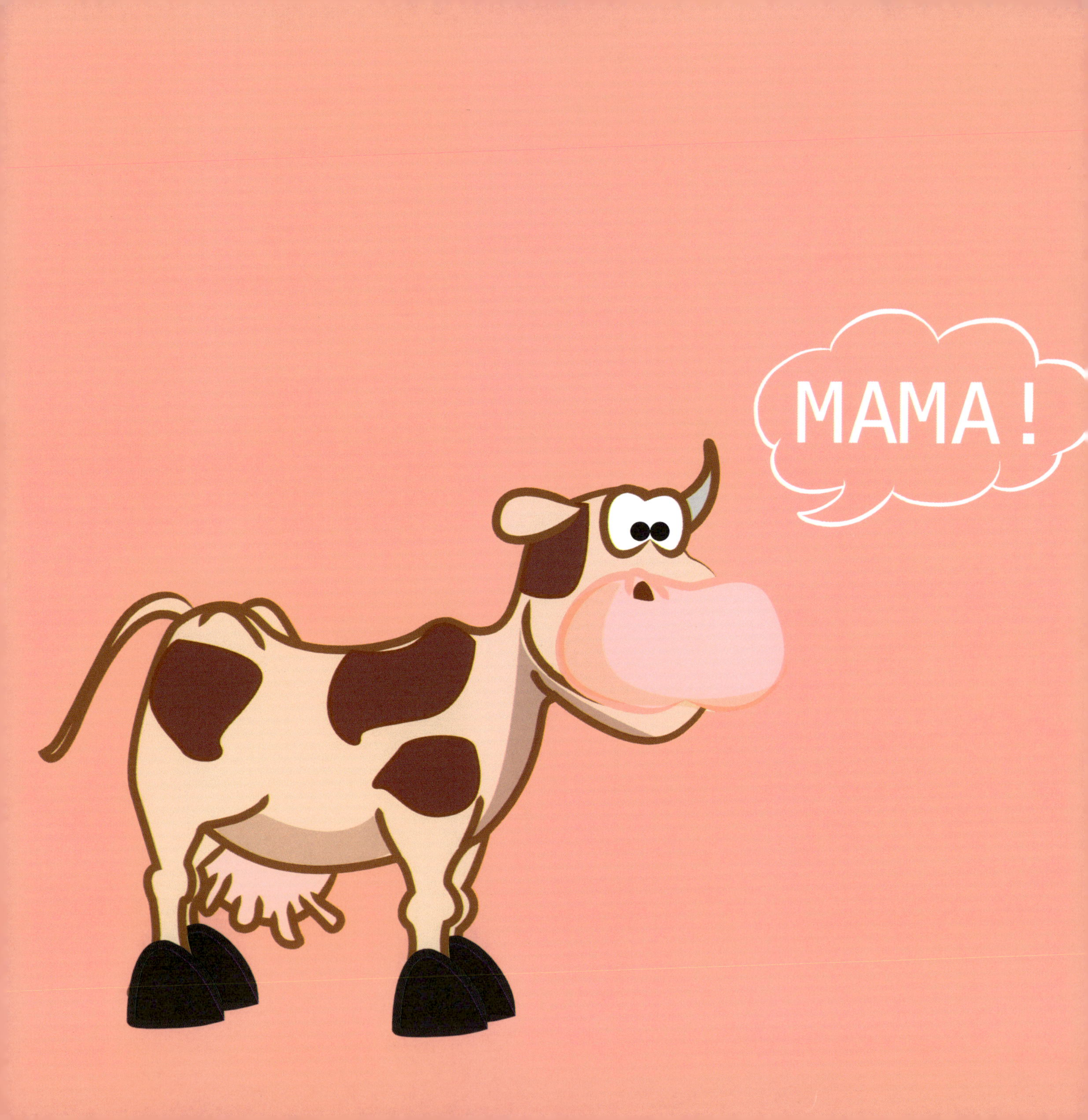
MAMA !

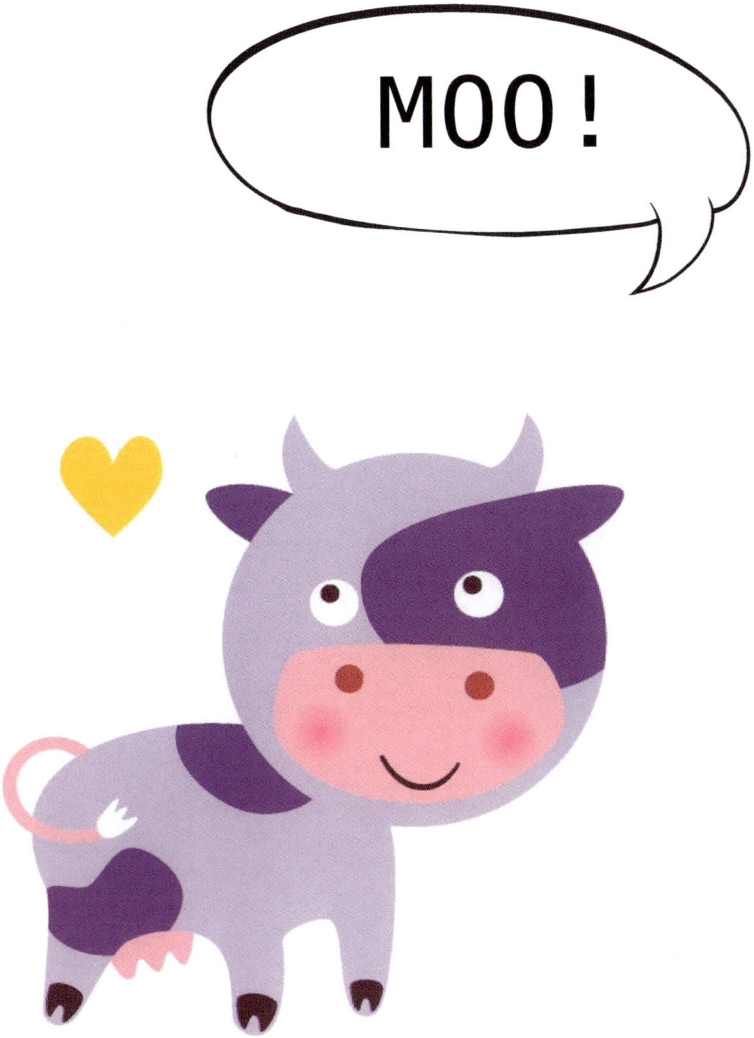
MOO!

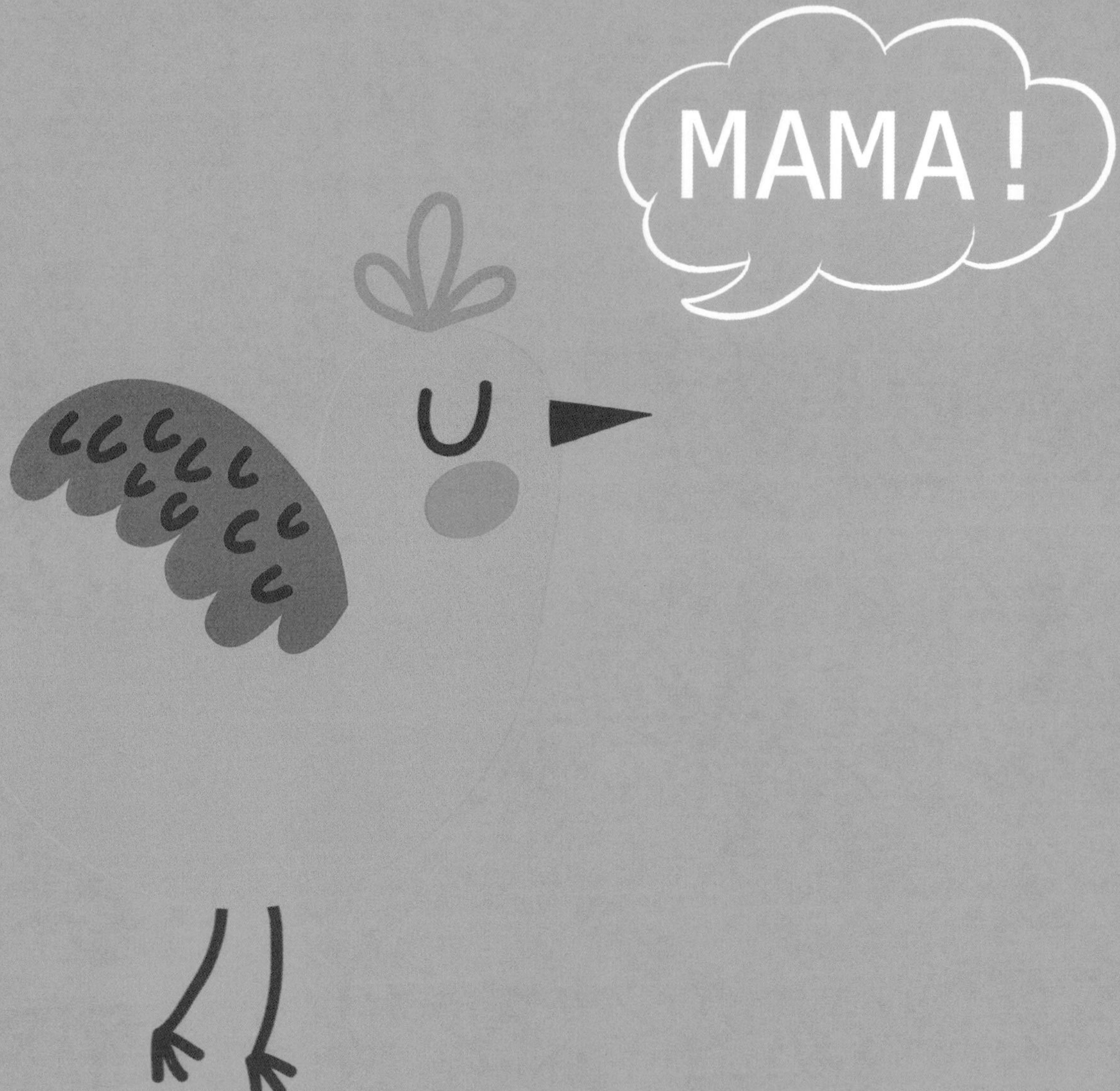
MAMA !

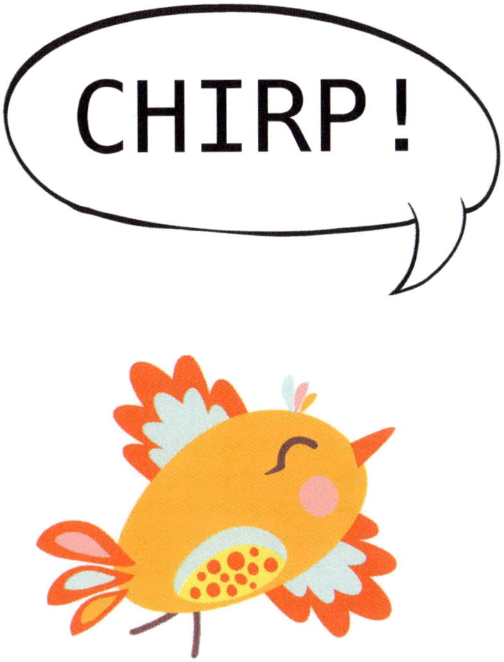
CHIRP!

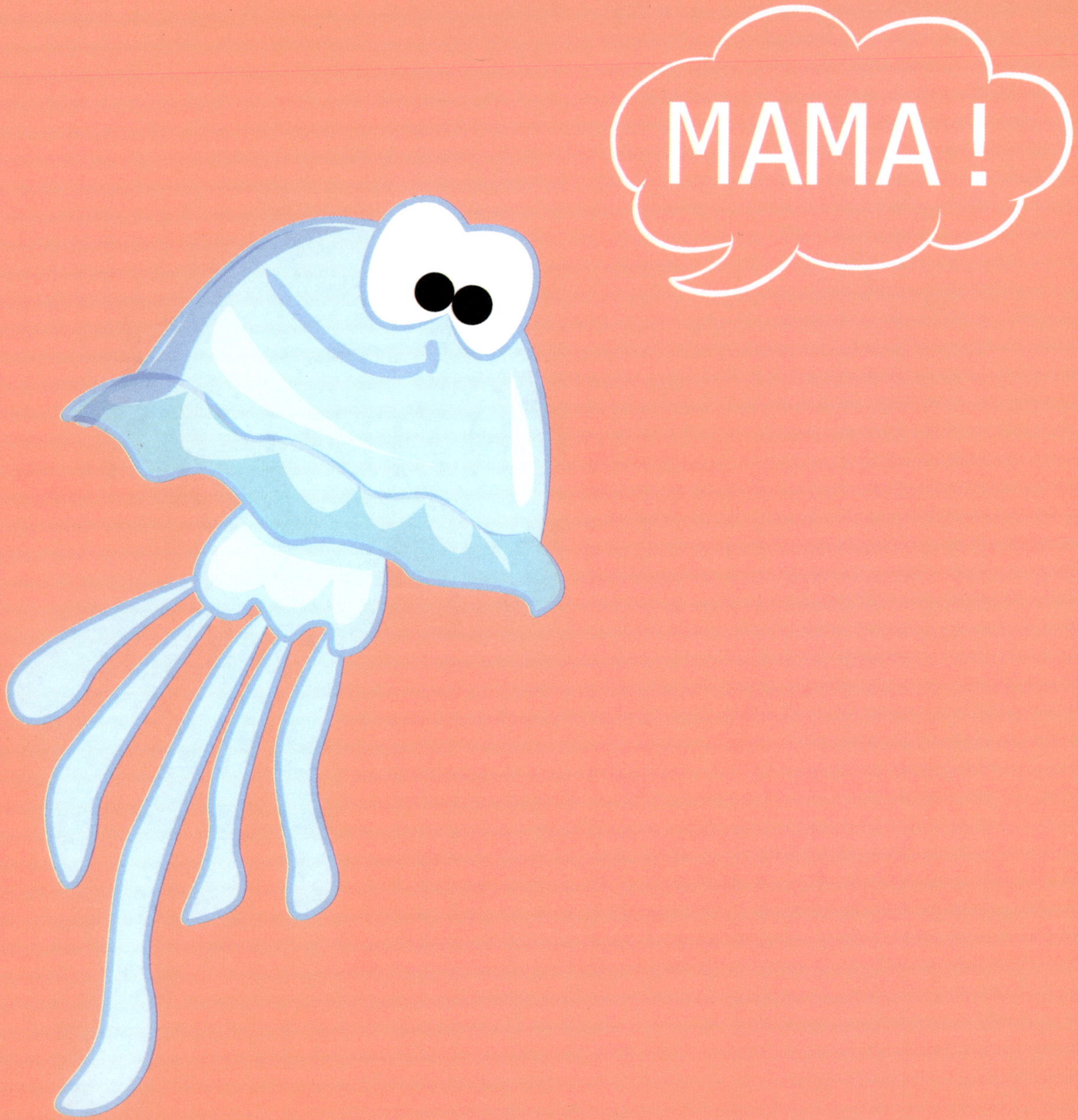
MAMA !

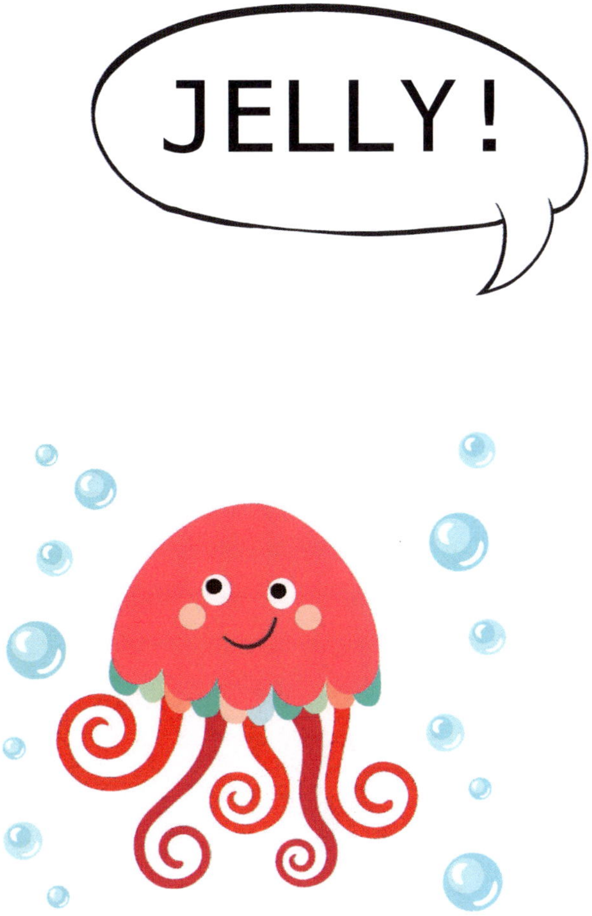
JELLY!

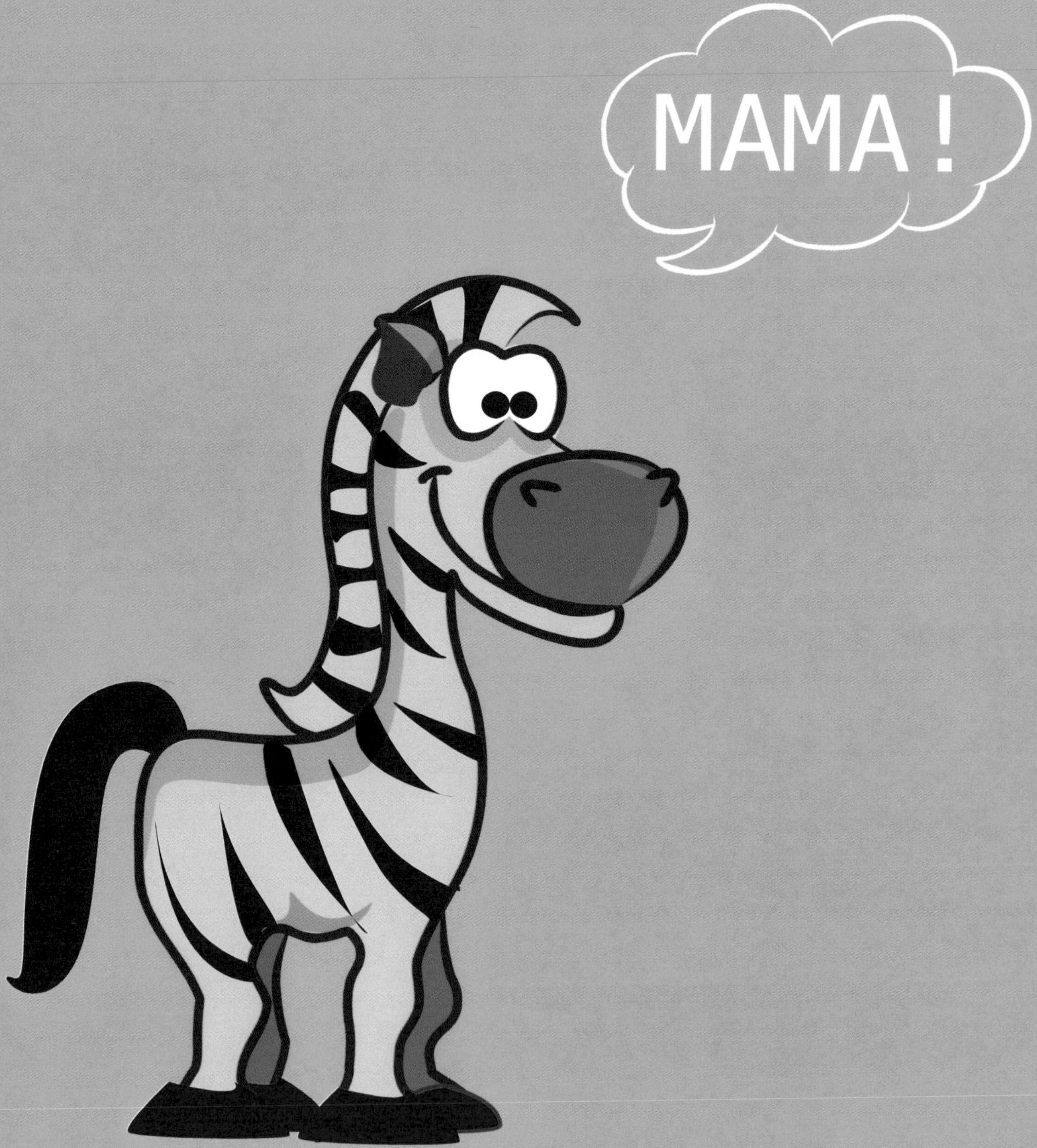
MAMA !

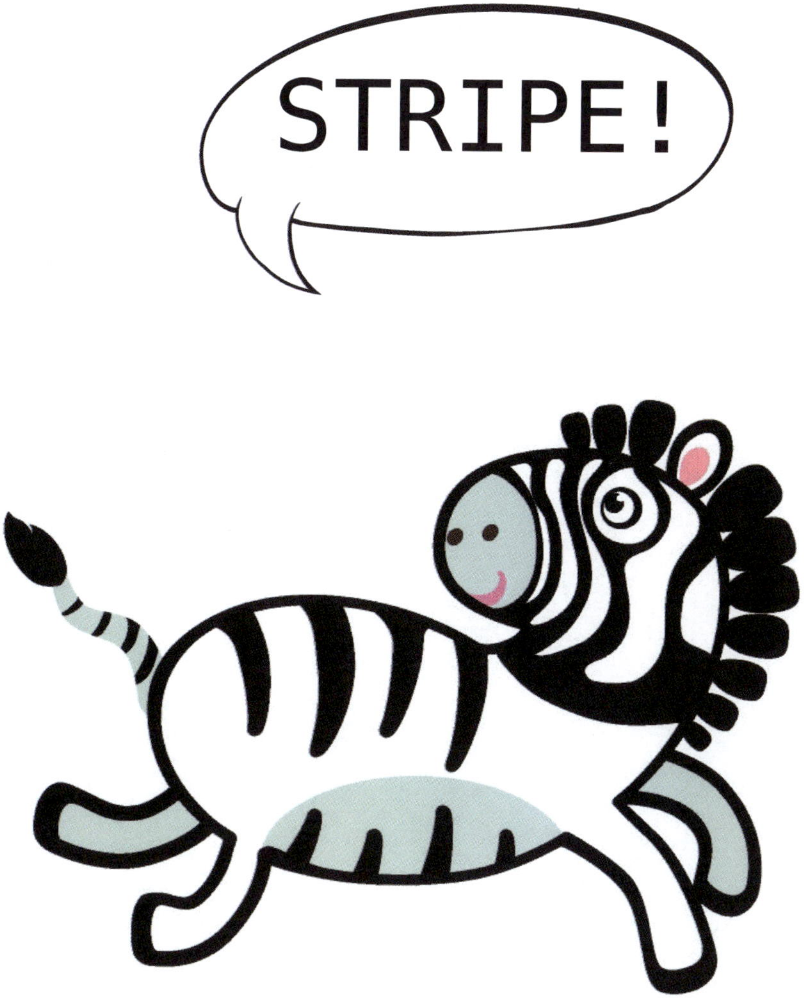
STRIPE!

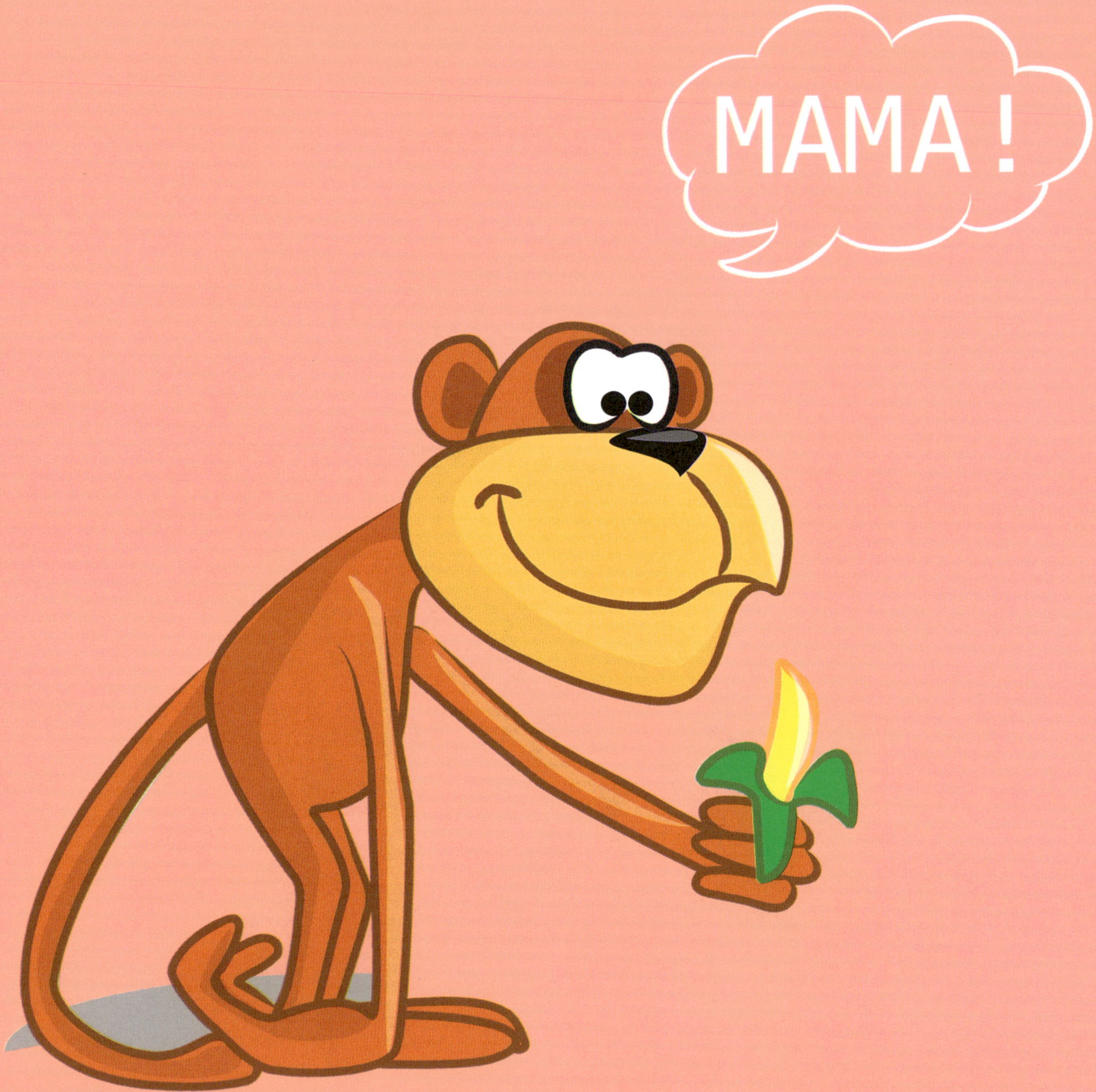
MAMA !

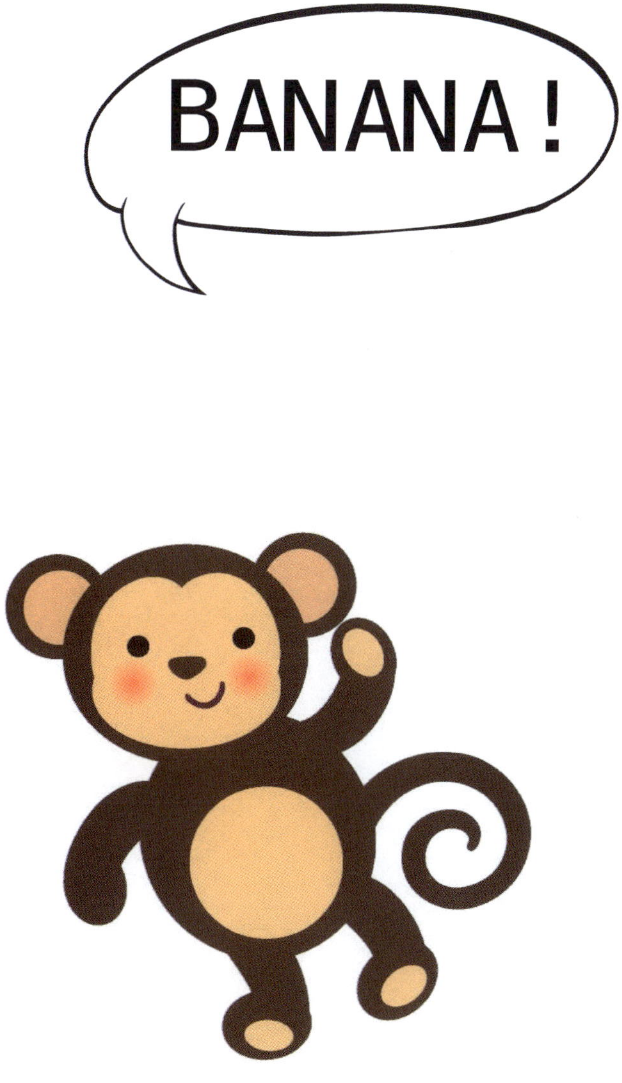
BANANA !

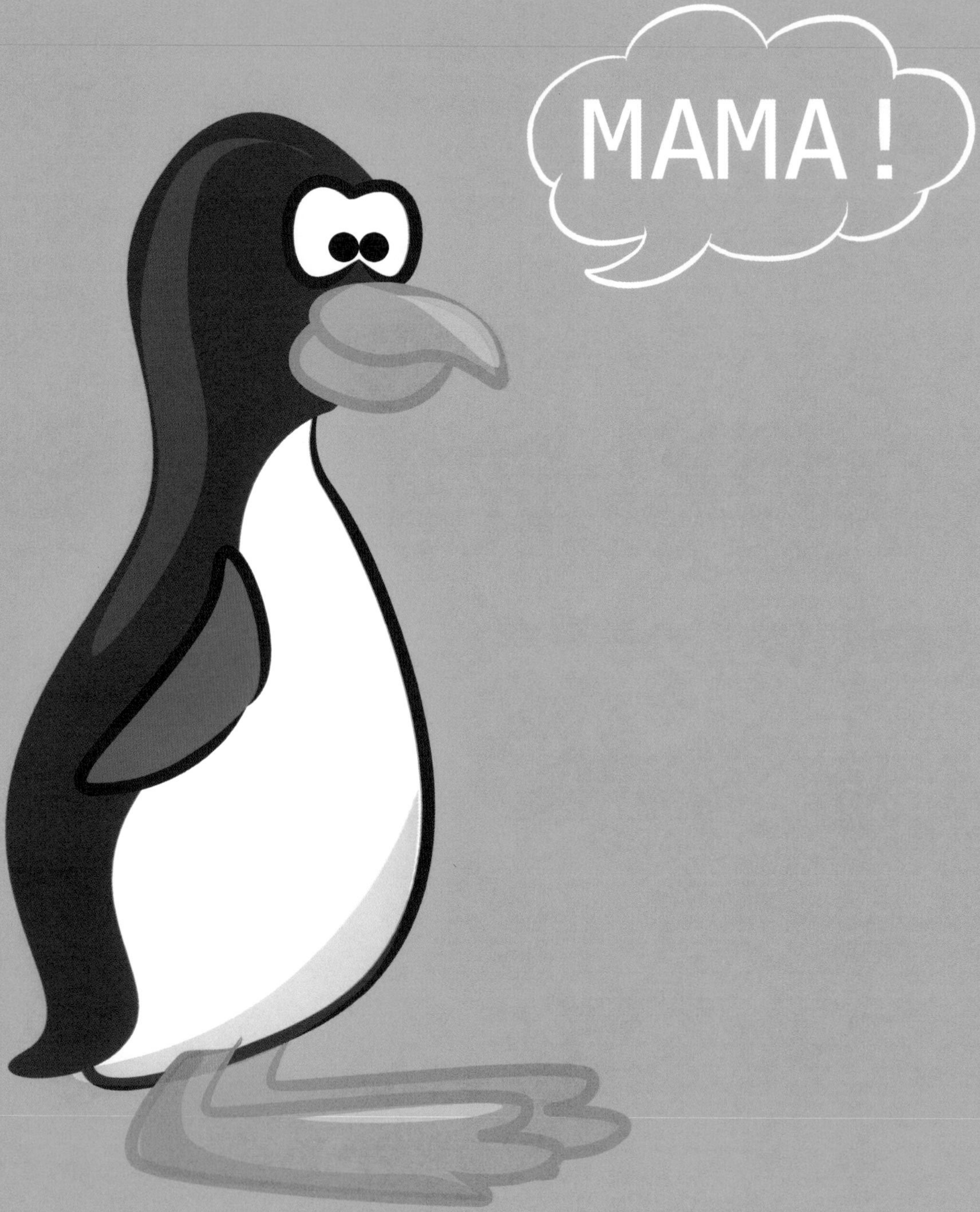
MAMA !

BURR !

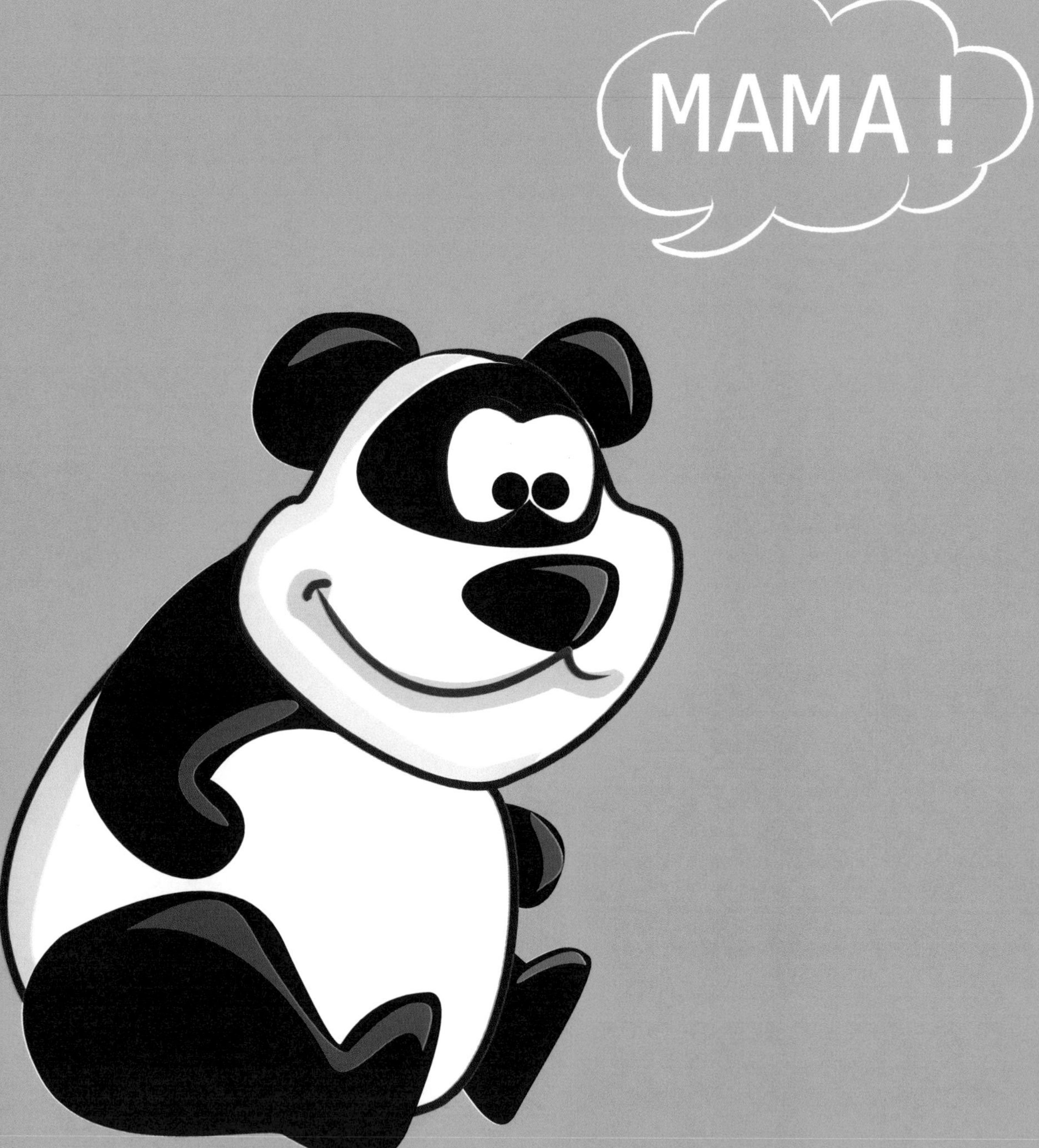
MAMA !

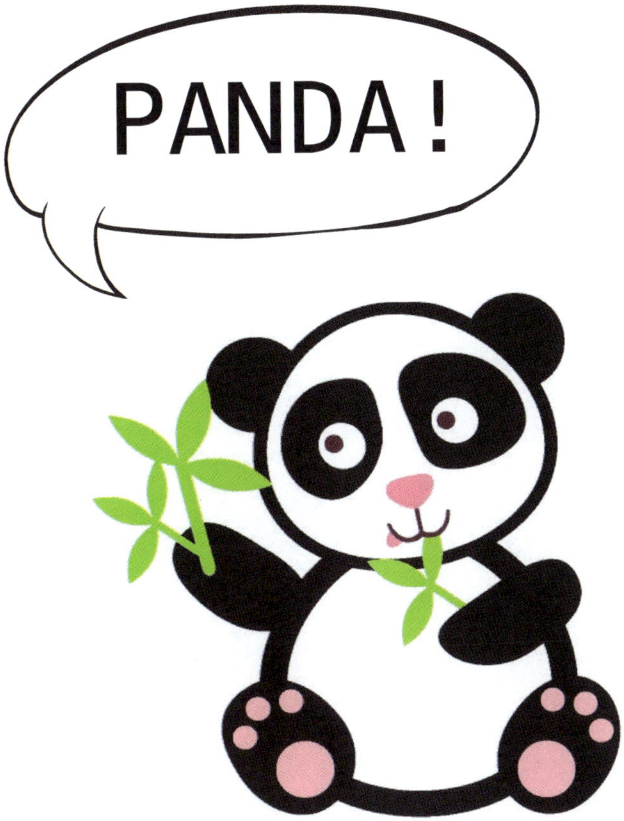
PANDA !

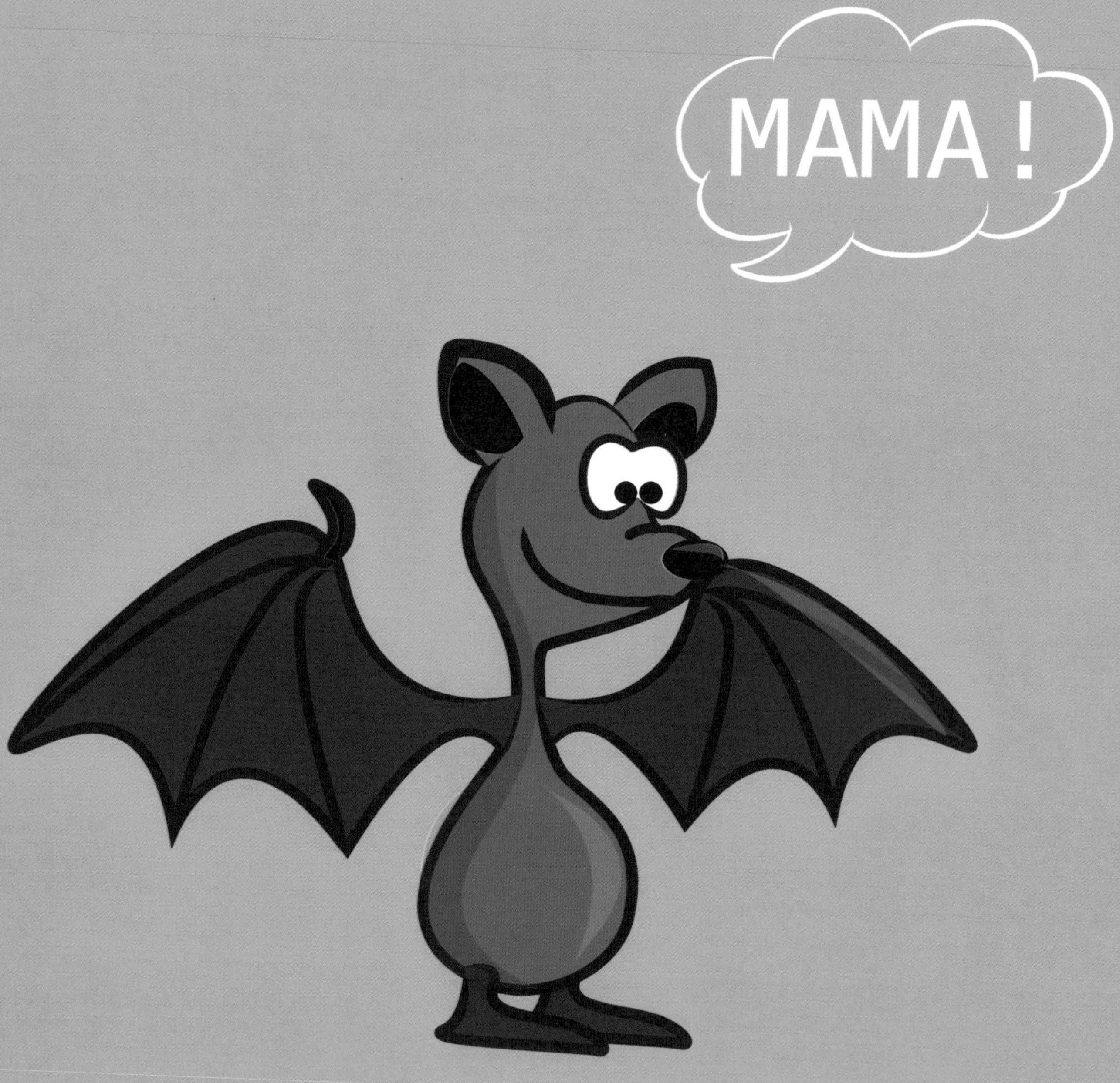
MAMA !

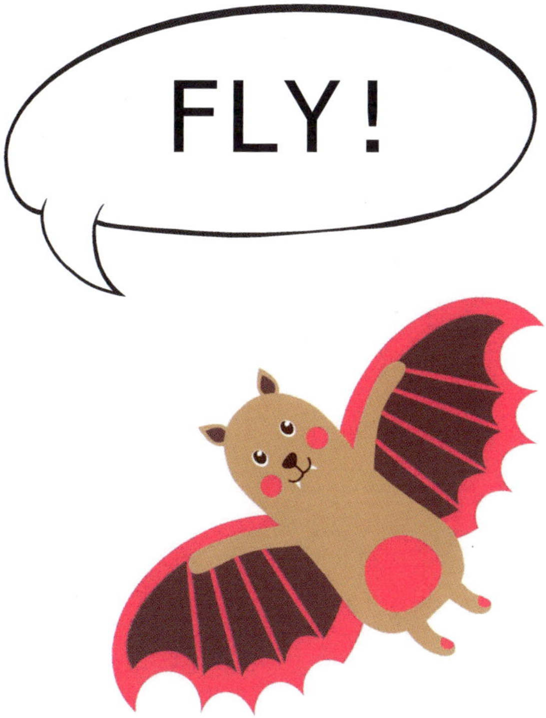
FLY!

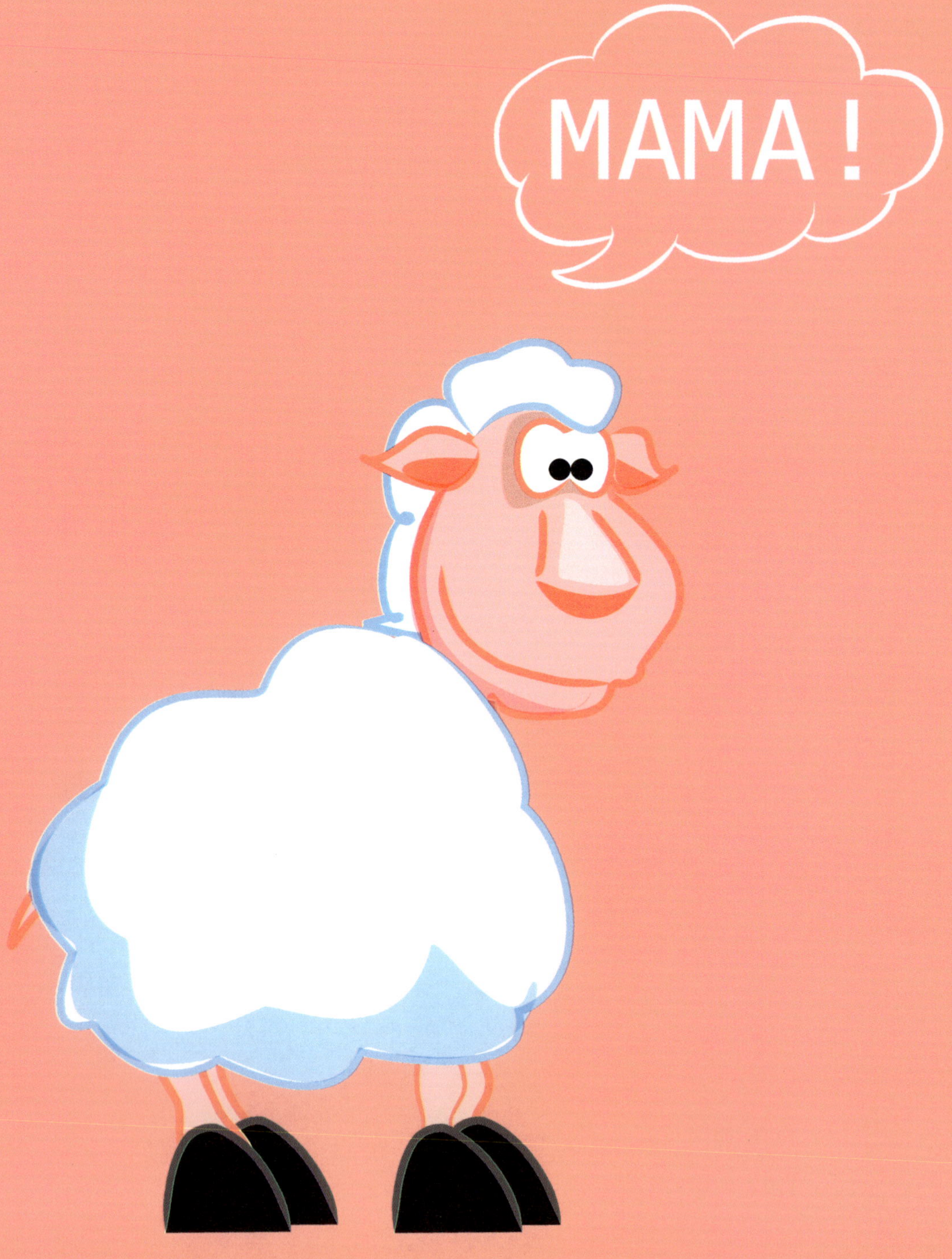
MAMA !

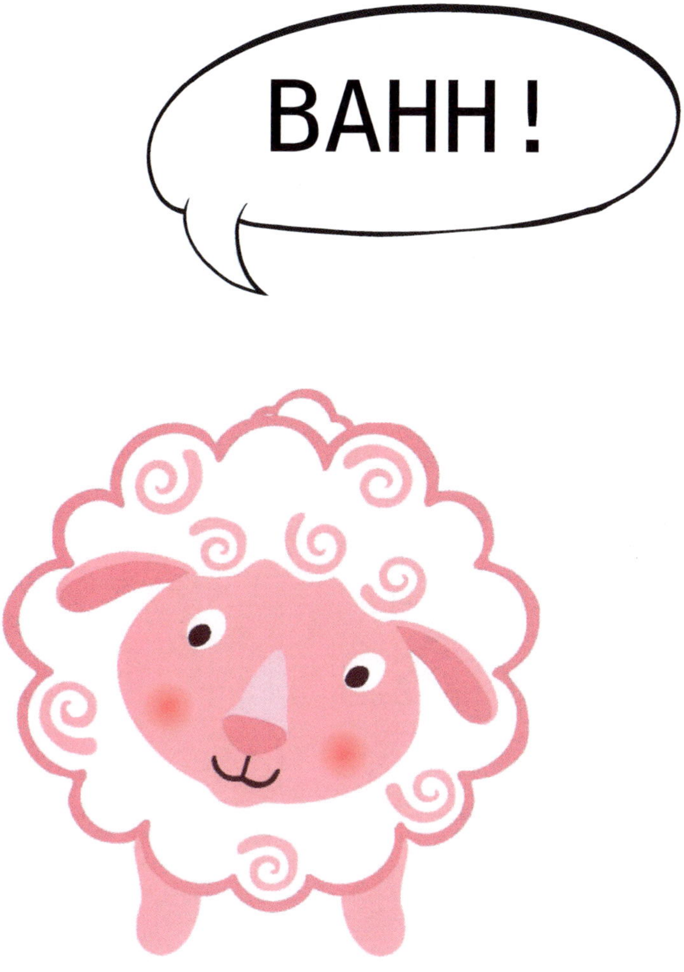
BAHH !

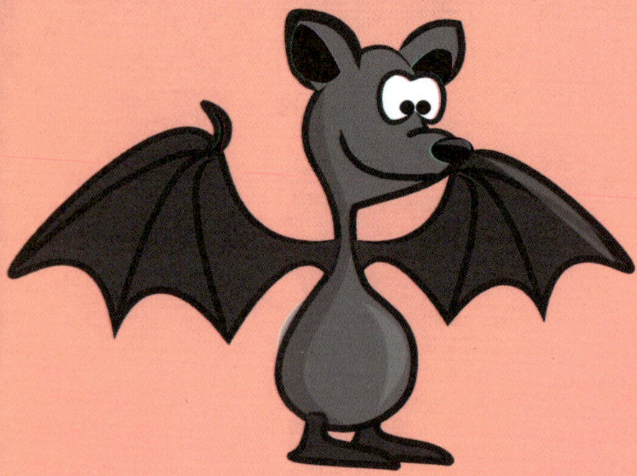
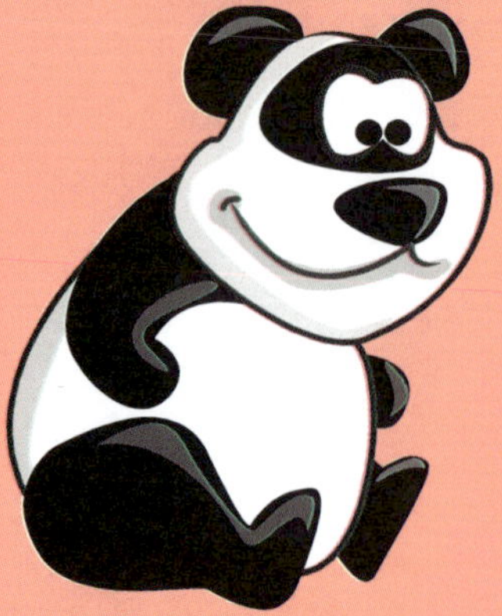
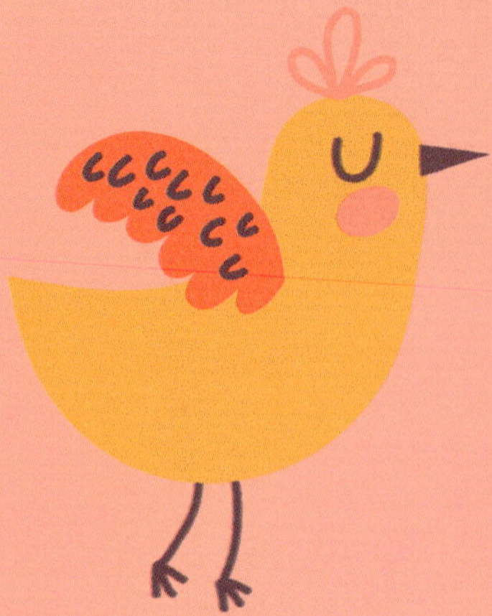
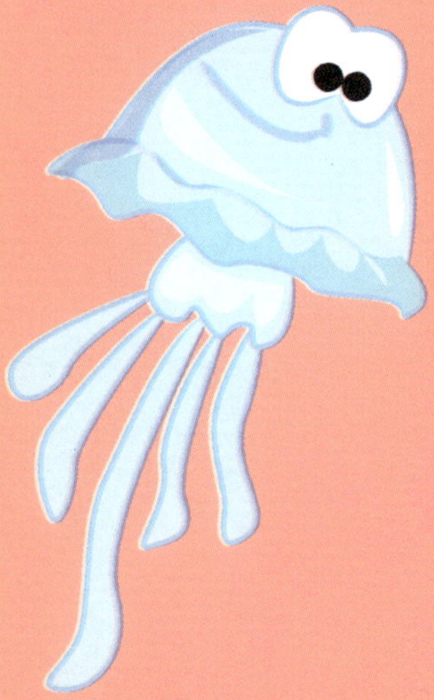
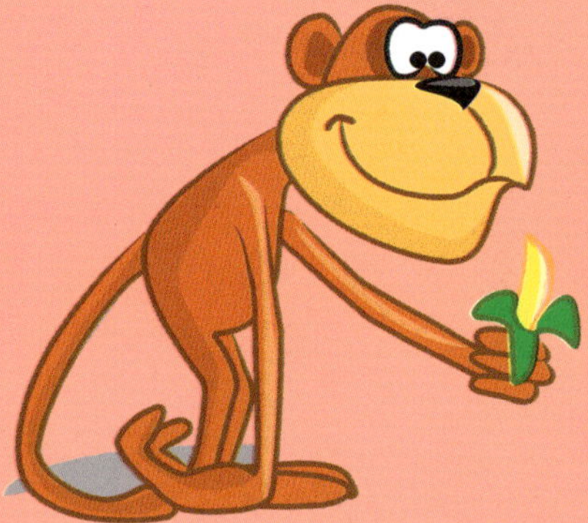
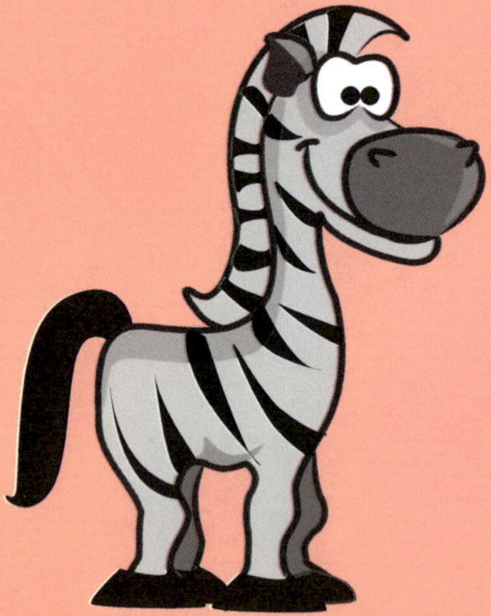
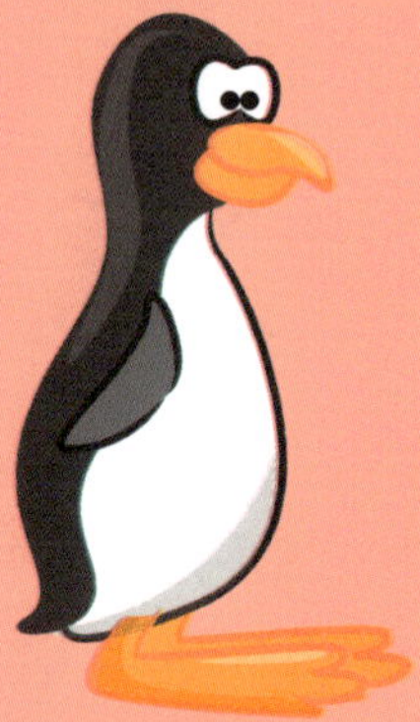
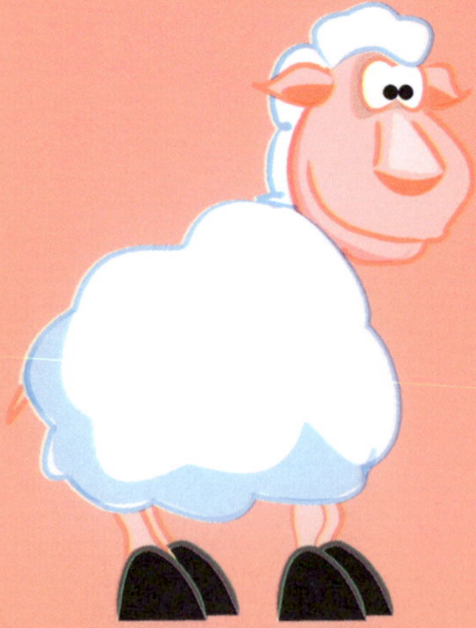
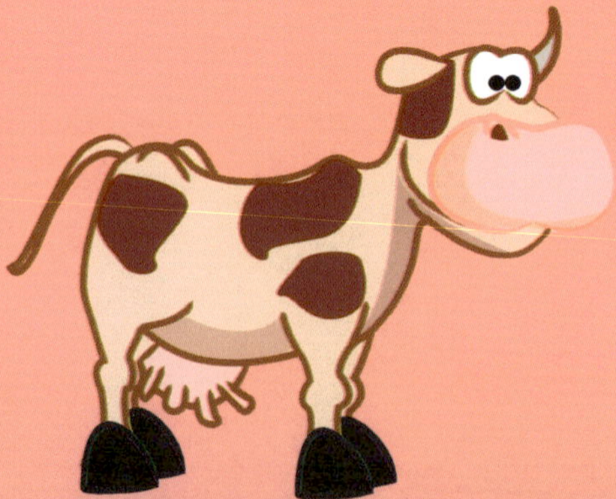
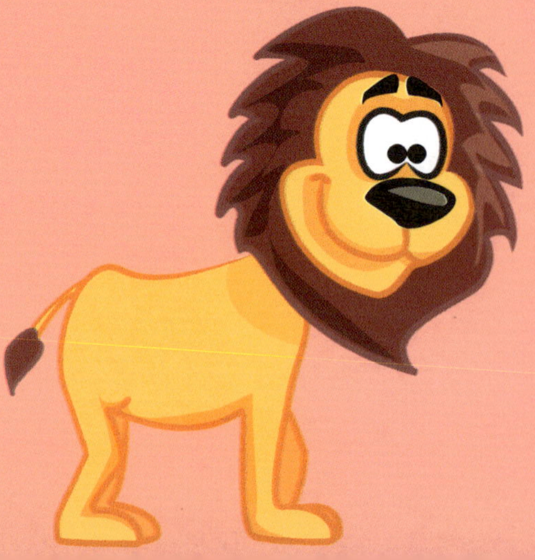

DADDY?

MAMA !

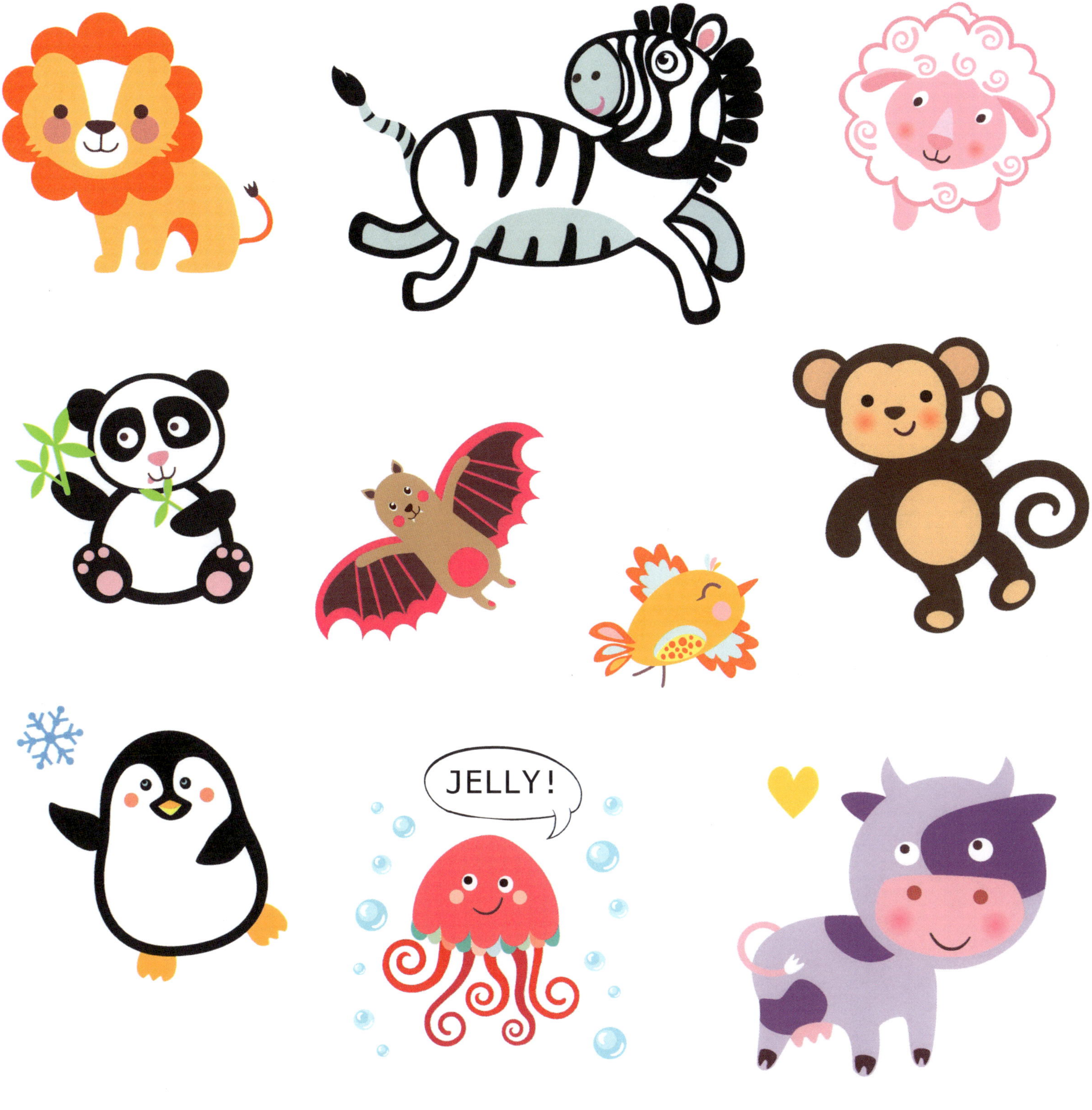
JELLY!

59066752R00017

Made in the USA
Lexington, KY
21 December 2016